Let Freedom Ring

John Winthrop
Governor of the Massachusetts Bay Colony

by Ed Pell

Consultant:
William Fowler, Director
Massachusetts Historical Society
Boston, Massachusetts

Capstone press
Mankato, Minnesota

Capstone Press
151 Good Counsel Drive • P.O. Box 669 • Mankato, Minnesota 56002
http://www.capstonepress.com

Library of Congress Cataloging-in-Publication Data
Pell, Ed.
    John Winthrop: Governor of the Massachusetts Bay Colony / by Ed Pell.
    p. cm.—(Let freedom ring)
    Summary: A biography of John Winthrop, religious leader and governor of
the Massachusetts Bay Colony, who worked hard and passed groundbreaking
new laws while trying to protect Puritan beliefs.
    Includes bibliographical references and index.
    ISBN 0-7368-2455-3 (hardcover)
    ISBN 0-7368-4484-8 (paperback)
    1. Winthrop, John, 1588–1649—Juvenile literature. 2. Governors—Massachusetts—
Biography—Juvenile literature. 3. Puritans—Massachusetts—Biography—Juvenile
literature. 4. Massachusetts—History—Colonial period, ca. 1600–1775—Juvenile
literature. [1. Winthrop, John, 1588–1649. 2. Governors. 3. Puritans. 4. Massachusetts—
History—Colonial period, ca. 1600–1775.] I. Title. II. Series.
F67.W79P45 2004
974.4'02'092—dc22   2003012123

Editorial Credits
Donald Lemke, editor; Kia Adams, series designer; Enoch Peterson, book designer
    and illustrator; Jo Miller and Wanda Winch, photo researchers; Eric Kudalis,
    product planning editor

Photo Credits
Architect of the Capitol, 41
Art Resource/ The New York Public Library, 6
Bridgeman Art Library/Massachusetts Historical Society, Boston, MA, 29
Corbis/Adam Woolfitt, 11; Bettmann, 5, 37, 39; Eye Ubiquitous/Paul Hutley, 9;
    Gianni Dagli Orti, 13; Robert Estall, 10
Courtesy Commonwealth of Massachusetts Art Commission, 21
Getty Images Inc./Hulton/Archive, cover; Time Life Pictures, 15
North Wind Picture Archives, 19, 22, 25, 27, 31, 33, 43 (top and bottom)
Photri-Microstock, 17

Table of Contents

Chapter One

Winthrop Arrives in North America

The New World was not how John Winthrop and the others had imagined. After two months at sea, they had finally reached the Massachusetts Bay Colony. Many of them were sick. Some of them were starving.

From the deck of the ship, they could see the small huts and houses of the Salem community. Huge forests surrounded the tiny village. The trees were dense and thick. The passengers aboard the *Arbella* had been expecting more. They thought plenty of food and shelter would be waiting for them. They were wrong.

Some of the passengers felt hopeless. Many of them wanted to go back to England. They could not imagine surviving in the wilderness of this new colony.

On June 12, 1630, John Winthrop, center, and other passengers aboard the *Arbella* reached the Massachusetts Bay Colony.

Winthrop and the other passengers did not turn back. In the weeks to come, many of them died. Others struggled to survive in the harsh environment. Even Winthrop's son Henry died shortly after arriving in the colony. Henry drowned while trying to retrieve a canoe from a nearby creek.

Winthrop and other settlers came ashore after landing near the town of Salem in the Massachusetts Bay Colony.

In His Own Words

In his first letter from North America, Winthrop told his wife, Margaret, about the death of their son.

Dear Margaret,

My son. Henry, my son. Henry, ah, poor child. Yet for all these things . . . I am not discouraged, nor do I see cause to repent, or despair of those good days here, which will make amends for all.

I shall expect you next summer (if the Lord please) and by that time I hope to be provided for my comfortable entertainment. My most sweet wife, be not disheartened; trust in the Lord, and you shall see his faithfulness.

Thy faithful husband,

John Winthrop

Winthrop was deeply saddened by the loss of his son. He also missed his wife, Margaret, and their family back in England. Winthrop poured all of this emotion into the letters he wrote home. In the letters, he revealed his sadness, his hope for the new colony, and his desire to see Margaret again.

Chapter Two

Growing Up

John Winthrop was born in Edwardstone, England, on January 22, 1588. He was the only child of Adam and Anne Winthrop. The Winthrops were fairly wealthy. Adam managed the family's farm in Groton, England. He moved the family there when Winthrop was four.

Soon, Winthrop began his education. He learned to manage the family properties, or **estates**. He also received an education from the local minister in Groton. When Winthrop was only 14 years old, he enrolled at Trinity College in Cambridge, England.

Love and Religion

While at college, Winthrop met a young woman named Mary Forth. She was also the child of a rich family. In April 1605, Winthrop and Mary got married.

Trinity College is located in Cambridge, England. When Winthrop was only 14 years old, he enrolled at the famous school.

The following year, the couple had the first of their six children. They named him John Winthrop Jr.

The new family moved to a small estate in Stambridge, England. The property was a wedding gift from Mary's family. Winthrop became a successful farmer on the land. Soon, he had enough money to buy his parents' house in Groton. Winthrop moved there with his family. His parents moved into a smaller house on the same property.

When Winthrop was four years old, his family moved to Groton, England. After he was married, Winthrop returned to this small town with his wife and family.

Things were going very well for Winthrop and his family. In 1613, he decided to return to school. He enrolled at Gray's Inn in London to study law.

It was not long before Winthrop's luck changed for the worse. Two of the Winthrops' children died at birth. In 1615, Mary died giving birth to another baby. Winthrop was 27 years old. He worried about caring for the family alone.

Gray's Inn in London is part of the four Inns of Court. In 1613, Winthrop enrolled at this famous law school.

Winthrop turned to religion for guidance. He became a **Puritan**. Winthrop and other Puritans wanted to get rid of Catholic traditions in the Church of England. They also believed in leading a good and simple lifestyle.

Starting Over

Six months after Mary's death, Winthrop married Thomasine Clopton. She was the daughter of a wealthy merchant. Winthrop hoped Thomasine would help care for the family, but she became ill and died within a year.

Soon, Winthrop met another woman named Margaret Tyndal. Margaret had strong Puritan beliefs. In March 1618, the couple married.

During this time, Winthrop was serving as justice of the peace in Suffolk County. He settled disputes and judged minor criminal cases. Unfortunately, this meant he had to travel away from home. Whenever he traveled, John and Margaret wrote letters to each other.

The Church of England

In the 1500s, almost all people in England were Catholic. The pope was the leader of the Catholic Church. In 1509, Henry VIII, shown below, became king of England. The new king got into an argument with the pope about divorce. Henry VIII decided to start his own church, called the Church of England. The king ordered everyone in England to go to this church. Those who remained Catholic were punished.

Many people felt the Church of England should be purified, or rid of all Catholic traditions. These people were called Puritans. The Puritans said everything should be based on the teachings found in the Bible.

Some Puritans believed they could change the Church of England. Others felt that they needed to break away and start their own church. These people became known as Separatists.

Chapter Three

Leaving England

During the 1620s, many Puritans in England were punished for their beliefs. Some of them were arrested, and others lost their jobs. Winthrop lost his position as justice of the peace. His farm was no longer successful. He began to worry about his family and their future.

In 1629, he joined the Massachusetts Bay Company. This trading company planned to start a colony in North America. Winthrop wanted to take his family to the New World.

Preparing to Leave

In October 1629, Winthrop was elected governor of the Massachusetts Bay Company. He urged other people to go with him to the new colony. Winthrop told the Puritans that a mighty work required mighty workers. He said that a good person could serve God anywhere.

Puritans in England were often punished for their religious beliefs. Some of them were placed in stocks for public embarrassment.

People had different opinions about leaving England. Some Puritans felt it was wrong to leave England during difficult times. They believed the problems would become much worse. Other Puritans were ready to take the risk. At least 1,000 people decided to go with Winthrop.

For the rest of the year, Winthrop gathered ships and supplies. These supplies included food, such as salted fish and beef, oatmeal, flour, salt, and vinegar. The colonists packed a variety of tools, clothing, and weapons. They also took 240 cows and 60 horses.

Winthrop looked forward to the voyage, but he was also very sad. He had to leave behind his pregnant wife, Margaret, and most of their family. Only his son Henry was going with him to the Massachusetts Bay Colony. Winthrop knew that he might never see Margaret again.

The Voyage

On April 8, 1630, Winthrop and other passengers set sail aboard the *Arbella*. There were four ships in the first **fleet**. Winthrop made the *Arbella* his headquarters. Even more ships followed throughout the spring and early summer.

In 1630, many Puritans in England left for North America. Some passengers rowed small boats to reach the ships offshore.

A Model of Christian Charity

While at sea, Winthrop wrote an important speech called "A Model of Christian Charity." It described his vision for the Massachusetts Bay Colony.

In his speech, Winthrop said that all of the settlers should help form the Massachusetts Bay Colony. He wanted everyone involved in building the new community. Winthrop told the colonists, "Delight in each other; make other's conditions our own; rejoice together, mourn together, labor and suffer together."

Winthrop knew these ideas were important. He said, "We shall be as a city upon a hill. The eyes of all people are upon us." For more than 300 years, these words have inspired leaders in America. On January 11, 1989, President Ronald Reagan quoted Winthrop in his farewell address to the nation.

The journey across the Atlantic Ocean took more than two months. Most of the passengers had barely enough food to survive. Many of them became weak and sick as the days passed.

On June 6, 1630, the passengers aboard *Arbella* were relieved to see land. Winthrop recorded the event in his journal. "We had now fair sunshine and weather," he wrote, "and so pleasant a sweet air as did much refresh us; and there came a smell off the shore like the smell of a garden."

On June 6, 1630, the *Arbella* and other ships in the Winthrop fleet arrived off the coast of Salem, Massachusetts.

Chapter Four

The New World

On June 12, 1630, the *Arbella* finally dropped anchor near Salem, Massachusetts. Governor John Endecott welcomed the weakened passengers. Many of the settlers came ashore to eat wild strawberries and deer meat. The Puritans soon realized that there was not enough food or shelter in the area to support them.

Winthrop quickly took over as governor of the Massachusetts Bay Colony. On June 14, Winthrop and the other new colonists decided to move. They settled in a nearby area called Charlestown. Unfortunately, there was not enough fresh water in this area. The settlers needed to find another place to live soon.

A clergyman named William Blackstone came to visit Winthrop. Blackstone had come to the area of Massachusetts Bay Colony in 1623.

John Endecott, shown at right, welcomed Winthrop and other
Puritans arriving in Salem, Massachusetts.

Blackstone lived alone on a small **peninsula** not far away. The Algonquian Indians called the area Shawmut, meaning "living waters." There were good springs for water on the peninsula. Blackstone invited Winthrop to join him.

On September 17, 1630, many Puritans moved to a small peninsula in the Massachusetts Bay Colony. The settlers named the area Boston.

In His Own Words

On September 9, 1630, Winthrop wrote a letter to his wife, Margaret. In the letter, he revealed his hope for the Massachusetts Bay Colony.

Dear Margaret,

I praise the good Lord, though we see much mortality, sickness, and trouble . . . We have had many occasions of comfort here and do hope that our days of affliction will soon have an end, and that the Lord will do us more good in the end than we could have expected . . .

Thy faithful husband,

John Winthrop

On September 17, 1630, Winthrop and the other new arrivals moved to Shawmut. They renamed the area Boston, after a town in England. When they arrived in the area, the colonists declared their independence from the Church of England. Winthrop and other colonial leaders signed the Church **Covenant**. This document founded the First Church of Boston.

A Harsh Winter

During the first winter, the new settlers became desperate. They arrived too late in the year to plant crops. The forests were filled with many animals and birds, but hunters could not get a clear shot. The trees were too close together. The new colonists had to depend on the food they brought with them. Much of this food was spoiled.

By February 1631, the food was almost gone. About 200 of the colonists had already died from disease or starvation. Luckily, a ship called the *Lyon* arrived from England with fresh supplies. Winthrop distributed the food and declared a day of thanksgiving. Also aboard the *Lyon* was a young minister named Roger Williams.

Roger Williams

In 1631, Roger Williams (1603–1683) arrived in the Massachusetts Bay Colony. Williams disagreed with Winthrop and other colonial leaders on many issues. He did not want political officials involved in religious matters. Williams felt that everyone should be able to choose their own religion. Williams also believed it was wrong to take land from American Indians without paying for it.

In 1635, Williams was arrested for his beliefs. Some leaders wanted to send him back to England. Winthrop told Williams to leave the Massachusetts Bay Colony. In 1636, Williams moved south to an area known as Aquidneck. He bought land from American Indians in the area and established the town of Providence, Rhode Island.

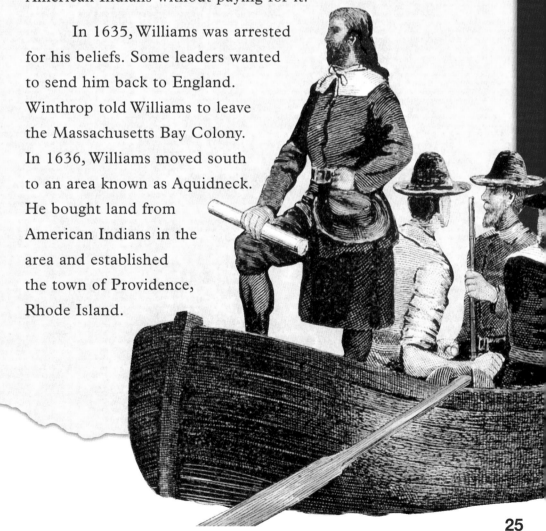

Even though food had arrived, many settlers thought that they made a mistake by coming to the colony. About 200 of the settlers got on ships and sailed back to England. Many of those in England who had invested money in the colony also gave up. Winthrop had to spend his own money to feed the colonists.

A Successful Spring

In the spring, living conditions in the colony began to improve. Crops were planted, and the weather grew warmer. The settlers also started building permanent shelters. Winthrop's knowledge and experience were valuable. He worked with other colonists to build a better community. In May 1631, Winthrop was reelected governor.

The large supply of wood in the area was used to build shelters and ships. In July 1631, Winthrop helped build the first ship in North America. It was called the *Blessing on the Bay*.

The *Blessing* and other ships made Boston an important trading center. These ships carried fish, fur, horses, and wood to the West Indies. Sailors traded these items for molasses, **indigo** dye, and cotton.

During the 1630s, Boston became an important trading port in the Massachusetts Bay Colony.

The products from the West Indies were traded to the Dutch in New Amsterdam for tobacco and fur. Finally, the tobacco and fur were traded in England for tools and furniture, which came back to the colony.

The Reunion

In the fall of 1631, Margaret and the children arrived in the new colony. Winthrop was excited to finally see them again. Unfortunately, two of his children had died that year, including his new baby daughter.

Winthrop's other children quickly became productive members of the colony. John Jr. was interested in science and business. He set up a saltworks soon after he arrived. A saltworks is a factory where salt is prepared for sale. This was good for the colonists, since salt was expensive to **import**. John Jr. also became a powerful leader in the colony.

John Winthrop Jr.

John Winthrop Jr. (1606–1676) was born February 12, 1606, in Groton, England. After studying law in London, the first son of John and Mary Winthrop sailed to North America. In December 1631, John Jr. was elected an assistant to the Massachusetts Bay Colony. John Jr. became known as a great political leader. He helped establish Connecticut and became governor of that colony in 1657. John Jr. served as governor of Connecticut until his death on April 5, 1676.

Chapter Five

The Massachusetts Bay Colony

The first settlers of the Massachusetts Bay Colony were Puritans. As the colony began to grow and improve, more settlers arrived from England. Many of the new settlers were not Puritans. Some of them were not even religious.

Winthrop and the other leaders passed laws to prevent problems in the colony. Everyone was required to attend church on Sundays. Swearing and fighting were strictly forbidden. Sometimes people who committed severe crimes were executed. Many people were **banished,** or told to leave the colony forever.

These punishments did not stop people from speaking out against the government. Roger Williams disagreed with the leaders of the Massachusetts Bay Colony on many issues. He did not want political officials involved in religious matters.

Puritans in the Massachusetts Bay Colony often walked to church. They were required to attend church services on Sundays.

Anne Hutchinson

Anne Hutchinson (1591–1643) created conflict in the Massachusetts Bay Colony. She was a well-educated woman and mother of 15 children. Hutchinson held meetings in her home for women to discuss religion. She believed that God's laws were more important than human laws. Her ideas drew supporters from around the Boston area.

Winthrop and the other colonial leaders thought Hutchinson's beliefs were dangerous. They wanted everyone to follow the rules of the church. In 1637, Hutchinson went to trial for holding religious meetings and continuing to disrespect the church.

Winthrop and the other court members sentenced Hutchinson to banishment. In 1638, she moved to the area of Rhode Island and helped establish the town of Portsmouth.

Anne Hutchinson was another colonist who fought against the strict religious laws. She started meetings in her home to discuss religion. Her ideas became very popular in the Boston area.

During a trial in 1637, Winthrop and other court members banished Anne Hutchinson from the Massachusetts Bay Colony.

Winthrop and the other colonial leaders worried about the affect these people would have on the other colonists. They agreed that both of them should be punished. Eventually, Williams and Hutchinson were banished from the Massachusetts Bay Colony. Both of them moved to the area of Rhode Island.

Money Problems

After losing the 1634 election, Winthrop was reelected governor in 1637. He continued to be a respected and powerful leader in the Massachusetts Bay Colony. He was also very busy.

Winthrop hired a man named James Luxford to manage his money. In May 1640, Winthrop discovered that Luxford lost all of his money. Winthrop was no longer rich. He was deep in debt and forced to sell almost everything he owned.

Many of the colonists wanted to help Winthrop and Margaret. They gave them a new estate of 3,000 acres (1,200 hectares). They also raised money for the struggling couple. Within two years, Winthrop had worked hard enough to repay all of the colonists.

Spread of Settlement in Southern New England, 1620–1640

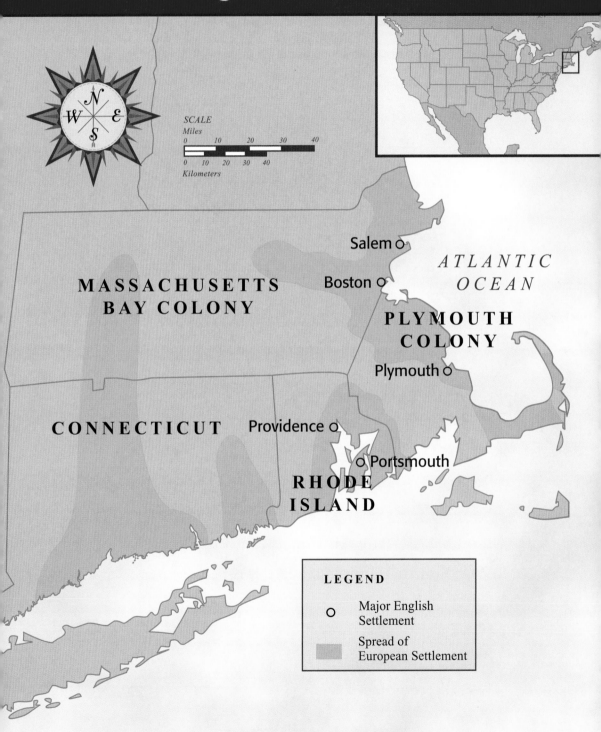

SCALE
Miles
0   10   20   30   40
0   10   20   30   40
Kilometers

Salem ○

ATLANTIC OCEAN

MASSACHUSETTS BAY COLONY

Boston ○

PLYMOUTH COLONY

Plymouth ○

CONNECTICUT

Providence ○

○ Portsmouth

RHODE ISLAND

LEGEND

○   Major English Settlement

    Spread of European Settlement

Chapter Six

Later Years

For the rest of his life, Winthrop served as governor or deputy governor of the Massachusetts Bay Colony. During many of these years, he was not paid. When the colony needed something, he often paid for it with his own money. He built dams, mills, and other public works. His financial leadership helped the fishing and shipbuilding industries get started.

Successful Leader

Winthrop also helped solve many foreign affairs. In 1643, two French nobles, Charles La Tour and Charles D'Aulnay, were fighting for the right to govern an area of Canada. Each of the men wanted Winthrop and his colonists to join against the other.

Even as Winthrop grew older, he remained an important leader in the Massachusetts Bay Colony.

Winthrop found a way to settle the problem. He avoided fully supporting either of these men. Instead, Winthrop made both of them feel he was on their side. He allowed La Tour to hire men and buy ships. He also continued to trade with D'Aulnay. In 1646, D'Aulnay defeated La Tour and signed a treaty with the Massachusetts Bay Colony.

Winthrop wanted to avoid any further conflicts with the French, Dutch, or American Indians in the area. In 1643, he helped form the United Colonies of New England. The union included the colonies of Plymouth, Connecticut, New Haven, and Massachusetts. These colonies pledged to help protect each other from outside attack. They also agreed to settle their own arguments peacefully.

In 1647, Winthrop helped pass one of the most important laws in American history. The Massachusetts School Law ordered every town with 50 or more families to collect taxes and hire a schoolteacher. Winthrop wanted education to be for everyone, not just the rich and powerful. Soon, other colonies in the area passed similar laws.

Education in the Colony

Winthrop and the other colony leaders were educated people. Many of them wanted to make sure every child got a good education. In 1635, they opened the Boston Latin School, shown below. It was America's first public school.

In 1636, the General Court of the Massachusetts Bay Colony established a college. The school was located just outside Boston in New Towne, which today is called Cambridge. A few years later, clergyman John Harvard donated money and his library of 300 books to the college. The school was named Harvard College. Winthrop and 11 others became Harvard College's first Board of Overseers.

The Final Days

In the summer of 1647, many people in the area of the Massachusetts Bay Colony became sick. Some of the colonists died, including Winthrop's wife, Margaret. They had been married for more than 30 years.

Less than a year later, Winthrop was ready to start over. He married a **widow** from Charlestown named Martha Cotymore. Soon, they were expecting a child.

Unfortunately, Winthrop would not live to see the birth of his baby. On March 26, 1649, he died at his home in Boston. Winthrop was 61 years old.

Even though many Puritans disapproved of big funerals, Winthrop's funeral was declared a public holiday. The colonists wanted to recognize his many accomplishments. Winthrop worked hard as a religious leader and governor of the Massachusetts Bay Colony. He used his power to pass groundbreaking laws and protect Puritan beliefs in colonial America.

National Statuary Hall Collection

A marble statue of John Winthrop is part of the National Statuary Hall (NSH) Collection. The NSH Collection is located in the U.S. Capitol in Washington, D.C. In 1864, Congress asked each state to donate two statues to honor important persons in their history. In 1876, Massachusetts honored Winthrop with a statue in the NHS Collection.

JOHN WINTHROP

TIME LINE

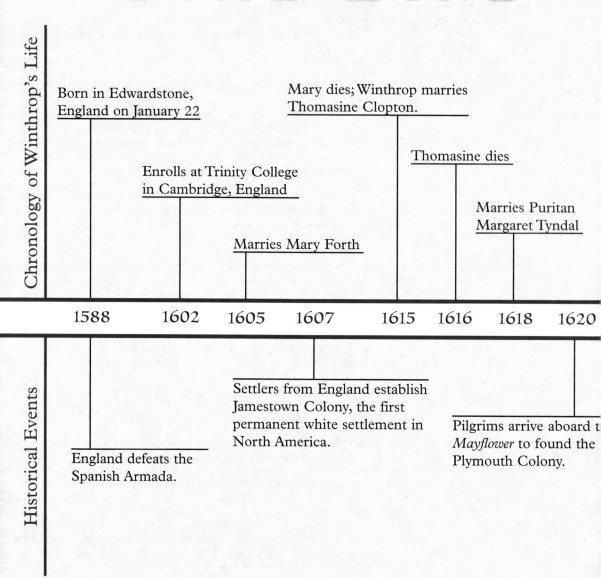

Chronology of Winthrop's Life

Born in Edwardstone, England on January 22

Mary dies; Winthrop marries Thomasine Clopton.

Thomasine dies

Enrolls at Trinity College in Cambridge, England

Marries Puritan Margaret Tyndal

Marries Mary Forth

1588   1602   1605   1607   1615   1616   1618   1620

Historical Events

Settlers from England establish Jamestown Colony, the first permanent white settlement in North America.

Pilgrims arrive aboard t *Mayflower* to found the Plymouth Colony.

England defeats the Spanish Armada.

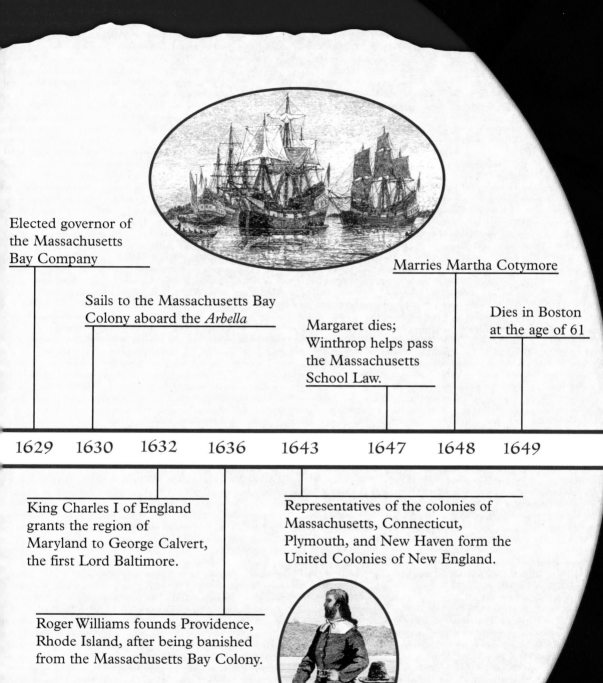

Elected governor of
the Massachusetts
Bay Company

Sails to the Massachusetts Bay
Colony aboard the *Arbella*

Marries Martha Cotymore

Margaret dies;
Winthrop helps pass
the Massachusetts
School Law.

Dies in Boston
at the age of 61

| 1629 | 1630 | 1632 | 1636 | 1643 | 1647 | 1648 | 1649 |

King Charles I of England
grants the region of
Maryland to George Calvert,
the first Lord Baltimore.

Representatives of the colonies of
Massachusetts, Connecticut,
Plymouth, and New Haven form the
United Colonies of New England.

Roger Williams founds Providence,
Rhode Island, after being banished
from the Massachusetts Bay Colony.

Glossary

banish (BAN-ish)—to send someone away from a place and order the person not to return

covenant (KUV-uh-nuhnt)—a written agreement or promise between two or more people

estate (ess-TATE)—a large area of land, usually with a house on it

fleet (FLEET)—a group of ships, planes, or cars

import (IM-port)—to bring into a place or country from elsewhere

indigo (IN-duh-goh)—a plant that has dark purple berries that can be made into a dye; indigo plants were grown on plantations for trade purposes.

peninsula (puh-NIN-suh-luh)—a piece of land that sticks out from a larger landmass and is almost completely surrounded by water; Boston is located on a small peninsula.

Puritan (PYOOR-uh-tuhn)—a group of religious people in England during the 1500s and 1600s who wanted simple church services and enforced a strict moral code; many Puritans fled England and settled in North America.

widow (WID-oh)—a woman whose husband has died and who has not married again

Read More

Allison, Amy. *Roger Williams: Founder of Rhode Island.* Colonial Leaders. Philadelphia: Chelsea House, 2001.

Connelly, Elizabeth Russell. *John Winthrop: Politician and Statesman.* Colonial Leaders. Philadelphia: Chelsea House, 2001.

Hodgkins, Fran. *Massachusetts.* Land of Liberty. Mankato, Minn.: Capstone Press, 2003.

Mangal, Mélina. *Anne Hutchinson: Religious Reformer.* Let Freedom Ring. Mankato, Minn.: Capstone Press, 2004.

Slavicek, Louise Chipley. *Life Among the Puritans.* The Way People Live. San Diego: Lucent Books, 2001.

Useful Addresses

The Bostonian Society
Old State House
206 Washington Street
Boston, MA 02109-1713
The Bostonian Society is Boston's historical society and museum. The organization collects and preserves the history of Boston.

**King's Chapel
Burying Ground**
Tremont and School Streets
Boston, MA 02108
For more than 30 years, this area was Boston's only burying ground. Many of Massachusetts Bay Colony's first settlers are buried here, including John Winthrop.

**The Massachusetts
Historical Society**
1154 Boylston Street
Boston, MA 02215-3695
Founded in 1791, the Massachusetts Historical Society collects and preserves historical documents and artifacts about Massachusetts and the United States.

Plimoth Plantation
P.O. Box 1620
Plymouth, MA 02362
A living history museum of Plymouth, Massachusetts, in the 1600s. Actors re-create life during the colonial period.

Internet Sites

FactHound offers a safe, fun way to find Internet sites related to this book. All of the sites on FactHound have been researched by our staff.

Here's how:

1. Visit *www.facthound.com*
2. Type in this special code **0736824553** for age-appropriate sites. Or enter a search word related to this book for a more general search.
3. Click on the **Fetch It** button.

Facthound will fetch the best sites for you!

Index